To the Archaeologist
Who Finds Us

To the Archaeologist Who Finds Us

Poems by Gary Thompson

Turning Point

Turning Point Books
P.O. Box 541106
Cincinnati, OH 45254-1106

ISBN: 9781934999288
LCCN: 2008937216

Poetry Editor: Kevin Walzer
Business Editor: Lori Jareo

Visit us on the web at www.turningpointbooks.com

ACKNOWLEDGMENTS

The author thanks the editors of the following publications where these poems first appeared:

Abraxis: "House," "At Night"
Bellowing Ark: "The Black Dog's Walk"
Beloit Poetry Journal: "The Book"
Benicia Bay Review: "How Did This Become That?"
Calapooya Collage: "A Talk," "Bouquet"
Chariton Review: "Settings," "Praise," "The Gift of Saying"
Chico News & Review: "To the Archaeologist Who Finds Us"
Clackamas Literary Review: "The Fathers"
Crate: "Charm," "Note to Keats"
CutBank: "Fallow," "Train"
Digging In: "In But Not Of"
Hubbub: "Three Men in a Boat"
Laurel Review: "Severn's John Keats, 1821"
New Letters: "Gothic," "This Morning's Shiver"
Mankato Poetry Review: "Rooster"
Santa Clara Review: "Opera"
Seattle Review: "Michigan"
South Coast Poetry Journal: "Mornings"
Suisun Valley Review: "Anniversary," "Port Orchard"
Tendril: "Babel"
Three Rivers Poetry Journal: "As For Living"
Windfall: "Sadness Comes"

Beyond Forgetting: Poetry and Prose about Alzheimer's Disease, ed. Hughes, forthcoming from Kent State University Press. Reproduced by permission: "My Father Calls," "Opera"

A Writer's Country, eds. Knorr and Schell, Prentice Hall, 2001: "The Fathers"

As For Living (chapbook), Red Wing Press, 1995: "House," "This Morning's Shiver," "Babel," "Before Christmas"

Anthology of Magazine Verse & Yearbook of American Poetry, ed. Alan F. Pater, Monitor Books, 1988: "Train"

Hold Fast (chapbook), Confluence Press, 1984: "Hold Fast"

for LK

TABLE OF CONTENTS

FRAIL GRAVITY

THE FATHERS

THREE MEN IN A BOAT

TEARS OR PRAISE OR BOTH

FRAIL GRAVITY

BABEL

Wintermorning. A man
and a woman and behind them
a creek that talks—
it does not murmur or sing.
Tears on the face of the man,
pebbles that need
to be found. The woman closes
her eyes. When she says *love*,
the creek finds a better word
that makes the distance
between them clear
as the crystals of air
floating above the water—
a cloud more sure and biting
than the fog that comes
from their mouths.

AS FOR LIVING

The dawn is dull.
I set all the clocks by your heart
beat, which was fast
last night; watched SAT
turn mechanically into SUN, then wound
my exhausted arms into sleep.
It's so easy to throw our hands
up in the air
at dawn and sit down and wait;
to close our eyes and let them fall,
the hands, where they may—
to wake up and rub our blue eyes
with the hand of a friend or the hand
of a grandfather.
Whatever happens, we *do* wake up,
and the childhood scar is gone. It stares
from the sky, the morning star.
Christ, it's so easy to go away
and never leave,
to move the body and save the dream.
To wake up tired in the sand,
sip wine, fall back,
and let the waves pump a life,
like salt, through our bloodstreams.
You see, dear, it's easy.
And if there is anything harsh
or grizzly or distant to clean up, well…
      the servants can do that.

THIS MORNING'S SHIVER

It turns out we were made small
animals shivering
over this earth with hearts
that pump blue stars.
Our frail gravity, at birth,
was buried like seeds in our eyes.
That is our right.
In the dark, we move our arms
around, panting,
searching wherever we go,
musky air, a wood softened by coffins,
a night pillow of breast. The rust
colored roots in the eyes
spread out coastal through morning fog.
Do the roots push inward or out?
At sunrise, a pelican flies south,
a shivering white voice breaks
into moan under palm trees.
        A frond drops and never touches ground.
No we don't understand much, but
this kiss—
one diamond from the inward blue
star of the earth
that shatters whenever another man's
arm comes near.

BEFORE CHRISTMAS

I go down
in spirits, these difficult days
before Christmas, like sand

sliding through the neck
that separates bottom from top
of an egg-timer. Inevitable.

And inaccurate, I know.
Forgive the bourbon in me,
ancestral and bottle,

sliding from pompous
to silly, bottom to top,
and days that sink or float

with love or without.
Forgive the bottleneck
in my throat.

GOTHIC

Against the lamp
lit wall,
the shadow
of your hanging
blouse
teases the learned
air.
In this dim
light, the book
dims
until Poe's words
blur
and the book falls
to the floor.
My hand is empty
when you come in,
wearing your sloe
eyes that slash
my world,
the eyes you choose
when we are alive
and go
at each other
with such tender
knives.

MORNINGS

A drowsy rain last night.
I wake early, mid-dream.
Yellow, tear-shaped leaves
stick to the window.

I sip black tea
and watch two squirrels play
in the stripped tamarack
against a wet sky.

The children dressed,
I tell about a grandaunt's
perfect griddlecakes
and stove wood. They listen.

After work, I open the letter
again. The words
are brittle and mean
an unsure future.

Do we sit down over dinner
and make lists that make
love better, more tender?
A calendar

with no seasons?
Dear, does it rain there?
Have the leaves changed?
Or just more of the same?

BOUQUET

Guilt, that time
I treated you I loved
badly, and found
I could not love again.

Our field, grief,
I have picked to hurt
poppies from,
colors crying.

Forgiveness, the word
that cannot come,
this vase
I bring of stems.

LULLABY

Winter soon.
The summer wane
too long to sprout
even our surface-
planted seeds.

Hushed eyes,
our whispered talk
about the child, her
nature, her left
and ghostly father.

In bed.
We, together, fall:
old goings, new
leaves gone
at first weather.

You breathe
your needs asleep.
Mine wait for snow
to cover them.
Mine brood.

A TALK

Now it's done
and your voice, crisp-
apple sound,

bites through the thick
skin my body
is lost in.

You want more
marks to mar
the withdrawn surface

of my face,
a last dangerous
chance

to find words
that will scar.
Dear Silence,

your stare is important,
like the knife
the child gave back

that hushed day
we tried to teach her
about trust.

HOUSE

There is room.
A man goes
to the window,
falls,
and there is room
to allow the falling.
He hums himself
calm, even on this dead-
end trail gravity
carves through the world.
No sadness
because there is room
to let the seasons become
what they must.
Do we push the storm
back into heaven?
Autumn was a success
or it wasn't, simply.
It is winter,
and there is a room
for winter.

IN BUT NOT OF

Winter seasons
the rose leaves
in front of your house:
first, dank
green, then black,
and in the cold end—
blue.
All winter
you prune. The weather
scars your hand,
cracks the surface
from blue wrist to work.
The salve
is a traced map
to the house that will take
you back in,
if you leave
your acquired skin
outside.

TRAIN

The sound *is* haunting,
lonesome,
even when it isn't
steam. We need the night
train's aching song,
still, to coax us from
the stillness
of sleep, to help us
recall the people
we left at lights-out,
and who left us.
We need this moving
and unseen train
to sound our isolation—
those who go,
and those left behind,
waving
in either direction.

THE FATHERS

ROOSTER

The eyes were red and big,
bigger than mine,
bigger than anyone's—
those rooster eyes
were red—red as the big beak
that pecked me, pecked my hair
when I turned and ran
from the barn, screaming
for my little-boy life
toward the screened porch
where the adults were sitting
in white Adirondack chairs,
sipping iced-tea and talking.
I was hysterical, crying,
the rooster squawking at my back.
I saw my father rise from his chair,
cross to the screen door
and open it, just as I slammed
against the gray stairs.
He reached down, cool glass in one hand,
and hoisted me up
with the other. I dangled
from his strong hand,
while the rooster scratched at the gravel
below the steps, still menacing.
Then the women were all over me.
My mother smoothed me
into her arms and cooed.
Mrs. Schwartz brought me a cold drink.
Soon I was tearless among them,
the adults and their comforting talk,
the rooster back in the barn.

THANKSGIVING

After Dad's quick toast,
after my lordless-
and-looneytoons blessing
about the missing (newly-dead
father-in-law, snowbound
daughter, and good-husband brother),
and after the children finished
sticking olives on each finger,
after the cranberries were cornered
at the far end of the table,
and after the first fork hit the floor
and the first spill of milk,
after everyone said *yum* with their mouths
full of whatever made them say it,
and after carving the second side of turkey
to keep up with the teens,
after the green bean dish circled
the table twice and still looked untouched,
after the gravy was gone,
after the kids were excused,
after the adults yawned and went drowsy,
   Mom said the same thing, the same sentence,
   the exact same words she had said
   a few seconds before—
after the silence, after the shared looks,
after the concern hushed over us,
we said nothing,
we who love her,
we who are of the same mind as her.

THE NEWS

Most mornings I woke earliest
in our quiet house,
a pajamaed kid
too awed to stay in bed.
Shivery winter dawns,
it was I who flicked the furnace on,
unbolted the front door, and walked
out in the star-flecked dark
to fetch *The News*,
leaving sock prints in the snow
along the driveway. It was I
who pushed the Windsor chair aside,
turned the lamp switch a click,
wiggled into my secret niche
beneath the corner table
stacked with books, and snuggled
down to sound out words,
stories from the brought-in world.
My elbows propped on newsprint,
The News still holding a hint
of chill, I read and stretched
across the familiar scent
of carpet, my cold feet pressed
to the furnace vent.

HOLD FAST

A vulture rests
on a limb up the cliff almost one
thousand yards away from these glasses.
The swaying red leaf—
his blurred head—makes him easy to find
in the *Field Guide*,
makes him almost too easy for us:
Turkey Vulture.
We watch for hours and nothing happens.

Later a hawk holds
against the strong evening
bay wind.
My daughter screams
when the wings change, fold back,
tuck in.
But I am watching the fine wing feathers
twitch casually like fingers
in the silent glass.
She already knows when the hawk
dives into her smallness,
a field mouse will be clinging stiff
to the only soil it knows.
Walking home in the near-dark
she takes my hand and we cling to our small earth.
She begins to sing hold fast,
hold fast,
hold oh so fast.

MICHIGAN

After weeks of living
too far inside himself,
the boy starts out
through ghostly winter trees
he has lived among. There is a hint
of moon in the mist.
Brief flurries of snow
dust the prints his feet make
and obscure the path
back to that safe sad place
where he stayed those weeks.
No fire now. A night
of freezing birds in his bones,
the lost faces,
the rolled eyes of dying animals
in what he calls sleep.
All night the sky snows down.
At last dawn. The world is blank
snow. No way back,
only out, if there is a meadow
or clearing out there.
The boy doesn't know.
There is only this snow
in the woods, and the tracks
he will make to go anywhere.

THE POINT

       where we both knew
we shared a point of view
about death and love, came
while standing at her father's grave
in Grants Pass, Oregon.
It was a dismal autumn
afternoon we'd picked
to return and pay our respects,
and the deodara cedar
she'd planted that distant September
her daddy died was wind-blown—
the delicate rosette cones
she loves, scattered on
the grave like decorations.

While she attended the headstone,
I wandered, read some
epitaphs, and invented living
stories so the dead might live.
But later, huddled under the deodara
when rain finally came, I held her
close, but kept silent,
for what would be the point
or use of words
at that moment, in *this* world?

DEAR CHRYSALIS

I enter the room
my mother has become,
dear chrysalis that she is.

I am a familiar face,
and hers a face of blue eyes
staring back, searching mine
to discover my name—
who exactly I am.

We slide by on silence,
the vaguely
awkward and re-lived silence
of a mother and son's
faint kiss.

Gary I whisper.
Her face empties slowly,
but then something flickers—
Oh Gary, she says,
and her eyes crinkle blue

in this moment,
the room we are in.

MY FATHER CALLS

My father calls from wherever
he's dead to ask about things
in his hesitant telephone voice
that can't quite believe
he's connected to me.

He's worried about Mother,
her evening shower, the outside care
I've arranged, the chocolates
she'd devour if I let her.
He's alive with advice, excited.

It's a common dream—
sons being summoned
by dead fathers—how the boy
in Michigan hid
when his just-dead grandfather

returned for their bedtime
story and goodnight kiss.
And years later, when there was only
numb darkness and a gun
and a bed lamp at his side, how that

reminded him to live.

THE FATHERS

They bake bread
late into the night,
needing kitchen smells, the lights
to overtake dread.

They look around
the empty room
with empty eyes, but doom
is not a sound

their ears can hear.
Sadness, yes, and loss
of some vague self across
a recipe of years

that came to this—
the fathers baking bread
into the night, the kneaded
dreams, the hiss

of steam, their children gone
into the night, and done.

OPERA

Hours after the botched conversation, I'm kicking
leaves on my way to the car. It's dusk and street
lamps flicker on, one after another, down the
unfamiliar block—a synapse I can see and follow like
a path back to the known.

I see now that when Michael mentioned *Madame
Butterfly*, the sophisticated nub of my mind false-
connected to *The Mikado*. But stranger, the part of
me that makes pictures, the side I trust and love, sat
me down in the audience of *South Pacific* and wouldn't
let me leave. My mother sat beside me, wearing her
Easter suit and green hat. Her perfume warmed the
theater for me. When she hummed "Bloody Mary," a
song she and my father listened to late at night after
my bedtime, I thought I glimpsed a flicker in the
mysterious dark of adult love.

So when Michael said, "It's opera," and Arika and
Steve agreed gently, I stared dumbly into the
disconnected air, scared, unable to click the lights
back on up the aisle to the exit.

AUSPICIOUS LIFE

1.
Admit you watched birds
to glimpse some inkling of a next life
the way the Romans did,
dissecting the sky and tracing
flights of geese through each quarter
to augur the future.

2.
Was it Michigan or a childhood
dream? You nestled in grandma's lap,
watching your first cardinals
in the snow-covered feeder
pecking at suet you helped grandpa
make, right in that sleepy kitchen.

3.
Yes, you watched birds, and once gods
fell earthward when you were young,
there were still orioles,
finches, and kinglets to carry gold
into the sky, still wings and songs
to rise, years to divine.

4.
In that mid-life twilight
when the bald eagle flew low
between the boughs of dense coastal forest
without waver, while you wandered
lost in dank shadow—wasn't that
a wing you wanted to follow?

5.
Assume the worst—this world
unwinged—and you envision Virgil's
hell, the entrance guarded
by a lake of fumes that kills
every winged thing, a place
without birds, or the idea of birds.

6.
Now, any angel you hold
yourself up to must be avian,
with wings so weathered, so laced
with loss, that you would rise
from your carved-granite life, over the gray
Pacific, never dreaming of heaven.

THREE MEN IN A BOAT

TO THE ARCHAEOLOGIST WHO FINDS US

We used language
up. Words broke
or collected decades of dust
and had to be trucked
off to the dump
with the rest of our refuse.
Lovely words—
    Abracadabra Bonanza
    Candescent Doggerel Eden
disappeared
from our literal lives—
    Fickle Grace Happenstance
Even our children stopped
finding fun in names—
    Ignoramus Jubilee Killjoy
stopped fish-mouthing
syllables—
    Lummox Molasses Nincompoop
    Osmosis Poo-poo
In disgust
words quit speaking
to us. They tip-toed around
our rooms
like despondent lovers
stuck with faithless
mates—
    Quagmire Rutabaga Stormtrooper
    Trample Umbilical Verisimilitude
In the end,
we were simply too busy
for words.
They shamed us

into a crystal night
of silence that seemed
darker than history—
  Waxen Xenophobic Yankee Zootsuit

SEVERN'S JOHN KEATS, 1821

Keats in his tiny body
is about to die. He shows it
in his eyes—heavy-lidded,
reddened.

He has dressed himself for death—
black frock coat, black
pants and shoes, white silk
blouse and bow.

His body, coughed nearly out
of blood, is almost lost
to shadows in the room,
but his graceful hands, face,

and the book he reads
still catch a glint
of languid Italian sun.
The cane chair he leans on,

and has just moved out of,
faces the window, soft light,
the idealized nature he loves.
Yet, he poses in the darker chair,

calm in his dissolving
into the shaded parlor
where leather books are shelved
up to the ceiling

and the great dead—
is that Sir Walter Raleigh?—

leave their human portraits
on the fading walls.

THE GIFT OF SAYING

My friend created Auden, an abstract
red-clay head whose features
and furrows grew so exaggerated
in the fire, that when pulled from the kiln,
there was nothing to do
but name it Auden.

Now in the midst of my growing
collection of fine-glazed
and intricate anagama-fired tea bowls
and vases, Auden poses
on his pedestal, a proud clump
of pinched-in face

with the gift of saying
those hard truths that clay can say.

THE BLACK DOG'S WALK

On our usual walk today, two juvenile bald eagles,
floating on the breeze, circled in and out of view—
first just above the cedars and firs, then the meadow
at the bottom of the hill, and finally out at Middle
Point, where the Cascades gleamed as a backdrop and
The Mountain, as you say, was most certainly out.
The morning throbbed with wonder, or so it seemed,
but of course the eagles were simply hungry and
hunting. What would Professor Olmstead make of
that oft-dreaded pathetic fallacy, my love? Still, when
we reached the clearing where the truck was parked,
there were six or seven of them wheeling high up,
almost out of sight, in the surely awed sky.

THREE MEN IN A BOAT

Three men in a boat—
one poet, one dying poet, one poet
who has lost his art.

Nothing happens.
No sinking boat,
no drifting for days
without food,
no choices to be made
about who lives, who dies.

Three men in a boat
simply fish, well
into a summer night—
some muffled words,
sandwiches packed from home,
starlight.

Whoo. Whoo. Whoo
of a deep-throated horned owl
unsettles the river.
The dilemma:
who should answer,
and to whom should he speak?

HOW DID THIS BECOME THAT?

I think you might stand up,
brush the Washington dirt
from your Pendleton shirt, cluck
your we-got-em-now chuckle,
and reach out your big soft hand
to take the money.
Take the money, my friend. It's OK.
But let's go fishing, get out
of this crazy place that keeps you dead.
Maybe the Trinity or Klamath.
You stuff the money in your old man's
wicker creel. I'll pack
gear, make some sandwiches.
It's been years, but we'll haunt
old places, visit the geezers, fish
until it all comes back to you.

I'll slip your last book
in my vest pocket, zip it into the empty
fish pocket waiting for fish.
That thick book with new stories
and old—some of the deepest and clearest
water you worked—feels right
in my hand, balanced, full of earned grace.
How did this become that
Hollywood shortcut
after you put the pencil down
and lay down in the ground?
"No telling," you say,
and we laugh

down the dirt road to the river,
glad to be this alive and near water.

                    for Ray Carver
                    Port Angeles

NOTE TO KEATS

There isn't much to say about beauty
these days, except that it isn't truth, ·
unless truth is glossy
and monthly. This is America

the goddamned beautiful
in the twenty-first century,
not Hampstead Heath
in the nineteenth, and we know

the bride is ravished
long before the bridal shower, the tree
logged off before autumn even comes.
Beauty is money, John,

and you know what urns are for.

FALLOW

A grave
is simple—
you find a maple,
dig a hole

between roots,
and allow the soil
to pull grief
down.

In fallow,
a grave seasons
words
to ashes.

Later, the maple
broadcasts,
as if the whole graveyard
were listening.

for Dick Hugo
Missoula

OUR HISTORY OF EPISTOLOGRAPHY

We began with memos
encrypted with intimate messages
we imagined our co-workers
could never fathom. We saw them
reading a plain English sentence:
   The pileated woodpecker sups seeds
   with its sticky tongue—
and thinking, boring ornithologists,
while we trembled, knowing
we'd be trysting soon in Cedar Grove
and you'd be wearing the red panties
I brought from Spain.

We tried succinct notes
but quickly progressed to daring epistles,
where we threw ourselves into words
with such heat we didn't understand
why the anonymous white envelopes
didn't flare up in the postmistress's hands.
Soon we were shipping sheaves
of hourly minutiae, the this-and-thats
of time apart: *The butterflies flew*
   back stainless from the dry-cleaners—
and we knew what that meant
to your maiden aunts who had quilted it.
After hundreds of pages, it clicked
that we were penning a novel
of letters. There was now a hero
who needed his stage to strut
upon, and a heroine who vamped
and swooned and carried on
like a 19th century sweetheart

56

of the heath. Our lives filled
with these other, more romantic, lives
and soon we couldn't tell
who was kissing whom
on the quilt in Cedar Grove
wearing the panties from Spain.

Finally, words escaped us
one warm evening in spring.
They got outside the fences
of our sentences and would not return,
no matter the honeyed sops
we left to lure them back.
We could hear them out there
in the dark. They were dangerous.
They knew more about the silk
and lotion of our intimate lives
than we did ourselves.
And that undid us.

TEARS OR PRAISE OR BOTH

PRAISE

Who hasn't been broken
by water and those
that take to water?
Praise American

widgeons, the alert covey
they become
in the protected coves
of Yukon Harbor,

each turning tail-up,
bottom feeding at low tide,
tail feathers
agape like hungry beaks.

Praise the delicate grebes
working rougher water
out past the point,
and the heavy-headed

mallards, the three of them,
two hens quacking
behind the haughty male.
Praise the kingfisher,

its loneliness,
the high-perched patience
of a christ
looking down.

Who doesn't break
into tears

or praise or both
when the truck horn blares

and the widgeons spook,
lifting off water
as one
taken to air?

JUST BEGINNING

My wife is almost as old
as I am, and we are just beginning
to hear the shush of wind
through the cedars in our yard.

It's a pleasing sound, this relaxing
into weather and the weathering
of such graceful trees.
The trill of a thrush pleases

us too, and the chatter of juncoes,
and the sound we imagine
when the robin slurps
another worm from the ground.

CHARM

This morning, the Scotch broom's sudden-yellow
charms the black dog off our usual path and into the
meadow, which also blooms with the more subtle
buttercup. The black dog and I lie back in all this
yellow, take our ease. Later, and all together it seems,
we entice two crows down to join us, but soon their
yawps and flappings add a manic beat that transforms
us all into exotic dancers caught in the spotlight of
this May sun.

                  Isn't yellow, in books, the color of
grief, and black, despair? How is it we are dancing?
Charm, I suppose, and charmed, and maybe it's true
that we—dog, crows, buttercup, and broom—are
mere trinkets dangling from the wrist of the goddess,
and she jangles us as she pleases, but aren't we
beautiful this day?

SETTINGS

Fierce coastal wind.
No one else on the headland,
only a drenched aura of no sound
but wind-blown
seafoam
against the diminutive flowers—
poppies, mustard, verbena.
The sun sprays
golden shadows across black clouds
into Vallejo's world
of *el oro de ne tener nada,*
and into our gold
of owning nothing in this world.

I do own one gold
on a broken ring finger
that César might envy.
His money was passion,
an unholdable love for unholdable things—
like these lovely goldfinches
darting off into the wind's crescendo,
tiny notes in a Beethoven Fifth.

SADNESS COMES

It inches in, drifts
like fog he watches cross the Sound
north to south. The man sits, dangling
his bare feet from the public boat dock.
Seattle, ghostly, disappears,
then Alki Point, the lighthouse beacon,
and nearby Blake Island he loves
to wish a life on. All is fog,
even the shore the dock connects to.
The air is water. It's like breathing
white rain, and it weighs his eyes down
to the waves beneath his feet. A fog
horn mourns somewhere in the channel,
soothing. Maybe he should row
his dinghy out towards the sound,
or maybe he should swim the fog
to find his island, so sacred
no one is supposed to live there.

TODAY

the clay just stays clay
in my hands—it will not become
a tea bowl or vase
no matter how I pinch
or coil or spit onto my palms
and rub for luck.

My uninspired hands can find
no form to shape
this chunk of moist gray earth
that feels transformed
and truer than the simple ball
of *Three-Finger Jack* I toss

back into its plastic wrap. Today
it is spring, official
now that morning NPR
says so. Still, there's a brush
of fresh snow, the sun-struck
melt dripping
from the tips of sword ferns
that grow in the loam
of moss along the craggy bark
of big-leaf maples,
their still-bare limbs
clacking in the wind.

ANNIVERSARY DAY

This morning we paused on an outcrop
and watched high Pacific waves
beat in, the surf plum red
from unseasonal kelp.
This afternoon we hold hands on a bench
beneath a wind-blown cypress,
watching Coast Guard boats
returning fishermen to the wharf,
and each ambulance driving off,
siren on or not.

PORT ORCHARD

Our neighbor, a man uncharted
by reason, borrowed his brother's
inflatable dinghy from the dry-docked yacht
at dusk and went fishing.

The little outboard puttered
across rough open water
to the lee of Blake Island
where he dropped his line in

and dropped dead. Gulls, the lap
of waves against the rubber hull—
his last imprint of this world? Or
the steady wash of tide

that pushed his tiny boat
into the charted sea-lanes out?

NEWCOMERS

Tall stem daisies favor the meadow
this year, the new black dog
and I discover on our first walk
up here in weeks. They're newcomers,
after somebody hacked out and burned
a small volcano of Scotch broom—
ash that turned an afternoon sky
bleak in late autumn. When the black dog
was dying that winter, we passed
this bog of slashed roots and mud
on one of her last walks
before I closed her old eyes—
a loss that holds to me like smoke,
though I know the black pup is eager
to please and today's unexpected sun
dazzles each yellow iris
of these fresh-eyed white wonders.

EVERYTHING WE SEE

My daughter wonders
why I have to name
everything I see,
why I sit by the evening fire
reading a field guide to trees,
when what could it possibly matter
whether the cone
we brought home
from our morning walk
was from a grand
or noble fir?

She knows
(or I believe she does)
that I'm no come-lately Adam
blithely handing out names
and claiming dominion
over the garden; and she knows
from her studious days,
that since Linnaeus
man has blessed all known
living things in the world
with Latin
cubby-hole names
that blur the connection
between the world of our walk
and words
into abstraction: no great,
no blue, no heron.

Unfair, I know:
Ardea herodias—

the Great Herod's heron—
an apt
allusion, I guess, but odd
that the great blue
is a New World bird
that only resembles the grays
of the Mediterranean,
as I confirm in an old guide
to Old World birds I rescued
from a box of winnowed
public library books.

My daughter jokes
about the old guide
coming apart in my hands,
sips her Merlot
and begins a story about her friend's
three-year-old girl
who will draw
a five-sided figure
and say "pentagon"
almost perfectly,
and at their grown-up
parties, she'll shape
her tiny fingers
like this, then sing
"My name is Lisa
and I am three,
see my pretty
isosceles"—the child,
my daughter adds,
of parents with way too much
graduate work in math,
and she laughs before going off

to phone the new man
in her life back home,
asking me
to re-stir the fire.

I drowse
into my chore,
then step out to the back porch
for more firewood
and stare at Seattle's lights
upon the water where Vancouver
anchored *Discovery*
in 1792, and sent
his first mate, Peter Puget,
off in the launch
to map this inland sea,
this sound that became his
namesake,
the Captain claiming landmarks
(mountains, islands, bays)
for King George III
using his crew's and British
naval names,
while leaving good rivers
to the Salish
tongue: Dosewallips,
Snohomish, Hoh—
rivers I love
to fish
just to say.

Any clear night,
a friend claims, two thousand
stars can dot

the black slate sky,
a braille
the ancient Greeks
could read easily,
but I can't pinpoint
one constellation
this cold night,
or recall a tale
about those sky lives
that might enlighten
my own, nor can I name
one star, though a few
are bright and waiting—
so I see simply stars
and black sky
with that big red planet,
Jupiter,
that keeps its kingly
red eye on me.

Star full
and cold, I carry
an armload of alder
back to the hearth,
rebuild the fire,
stir until it flames full
again, then pour
a fresh tumbler
of Tennessee
sippin' whiskey—
Jack Daniel's
Old Time Old
No. 7, and settle
into the *papa-body* chair.

Whiskey warms
the room while the fire
is humming
names, or so it seems,
of all the fish
that need my catching—
humpies, silvers,
kings and chum,
sockeyes, steelies,
cut-throats, jacks, and—
or am I just dreaming
the last-run ferry's
one long blast
that warns it is making way,
leaving the night
our own.

Now I hear
my daughter wander
room to room, upstairs
then down, in this house
she did not grow up in,
and when she returns
to the hearth, she carries,
as she always does,
the tattered family
photo album
from her mother's weathered
desk, and the rest
of the evening we sort
through pictures together,
putting familiar faces
and dates and places

back into our lives,
so that when we hug
goodnight, we are held
in the arms
of names we hold
in common.

Her name is Emily,
Amherstian, "so old-fashioned"
her great-grandmother griped
that autumn morning
she was born; and that tree?
—not noble, grand.

NOTES

"As for Living"—The title and last line are translated from the Symbolist poet Villiers de l'Isle-Adam's dramatic poem, *Axel*, 1890.

"My Father Calls"—It turns out the idea of the father's hesitant phone connection is similar to a situation in beautiful lines written earlier by a friend, Thomas Aslin, in *Sweet Smoke* (Redwing Press, 2006). I thank him for the subconscious inspiration.

"Severn's John Keats, 1821"—I have conflated events in Keats's life into this famous portrait.

"Settings"—The Spanish phrase, *el oro de ne tener nada* (the gold of owning nothing) is by César Vallejo in "Poem XLV" from *Trilce*, 1922, and is one of many Vallejo lines on my lifelong list of favorites.

"Port Orchard"—I realized shortly after I wrote this poem, which was "triggered" by an actual local event, that it was also a small homage to my friend and teacher, Richard Hugo, a remarkable poet who is too-little remembered twenty-five years after his too-early death. See "Salt Water Story" from his collected poems, *Making Certain It Goes On*, 1984.

Gary Thompson's poems have been published in a wide range of magazines, from *American Poetry Review* to *Writers' Forum*; several anthologies; and three previous collections: *Hold Fast*, *As For Living*, and *On John Muir's Trail*. He lives with his wife, Linda, on San Juan Island, and likes to think of himself as the novice skipper of a modest boat, an old trawler named Keats.

LaVergne, TN USA
25 August 2009
155916LV00009B/61/P